Taikan's
Alphabet

Taikan's Alphabet

by Jeanne Jeffares

C is for Canongate

A

is for angel, apple, ancient Athenian, athlete, ape and artist and anemones.

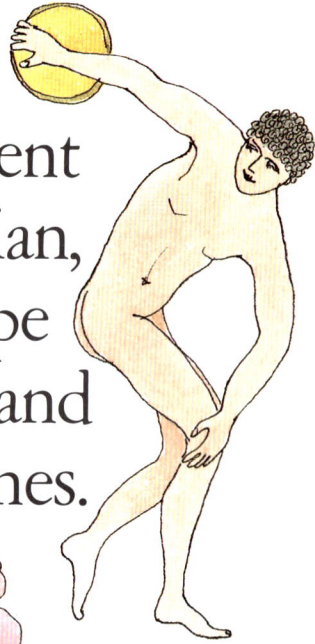

B

is for Babylonian,
ball, bust, boat, bow, banana.

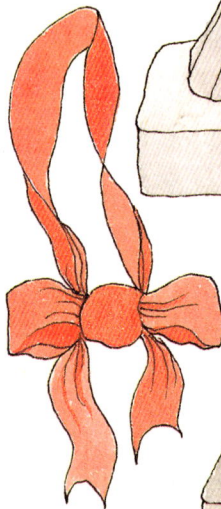

C is for

cockle shell,
crocodile,
cactus,
cherries,
conifer, cats
and   carp.

D is for ding-
dong
bells, dunce,
dromedary,
dianthus.

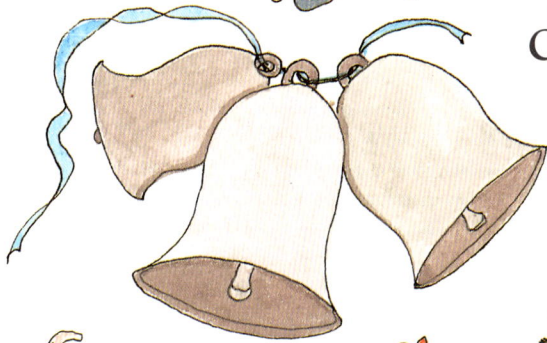

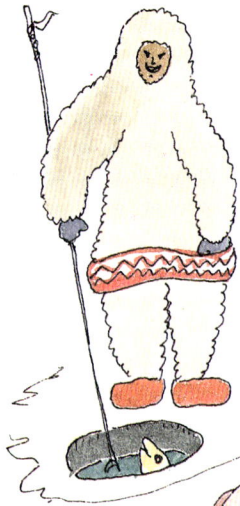

E is for

eskimo
and Eve

(in the garden of)
Eden, elephants
and eating.

F is for frogs, fishing for fishes, a fort, figs and for fairies.

G

is for

gondola, giraffes, garland,
gloves, grapes.

H is for hens, holly,

hippopotamus, helmet, hats,
hypericum, house.

I

I is for invalid, identical twins, Indian rope trick, immersion, Irish moss, ink caps, ivy.

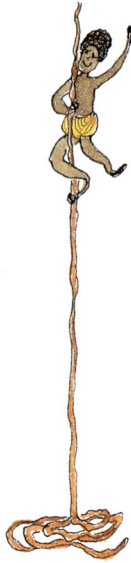

J is for jay,
Jupiter, Juno,
jugs

and
jam
jars,

jack-in-the
box and
jellyfish.

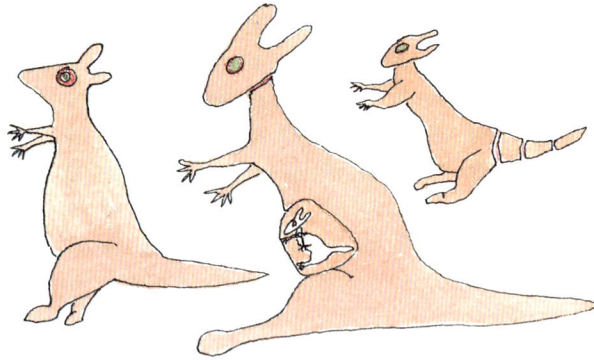

K is for kettle,

kangaroo,
kepi and
and kale,

king
kirk,

karate.

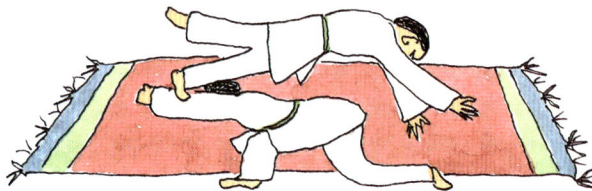

A Letter with Lots of Love from Lucy Locket

L is for

lobster,
llamas,
lemon
and a
letter.

ladder and liberty,

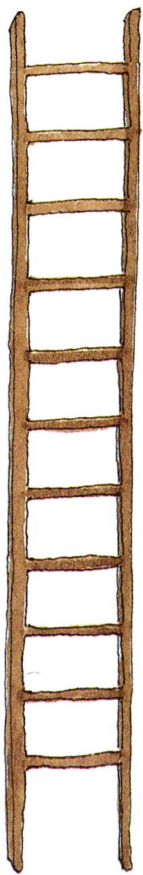

is for mangel-wurzel,
Madonna,
marigold,

M

magician,

A MAGICIAN.

mackerel.

is for Napoleon,

N

nautch-wali
and nasturtium,
Neptune, nest
and nautilus.

OBELISK.

O is for

Orion, ostrich,
octopus, obelisk
and olive branch.

P

is for

patchwork quilt,

pail and

panda,

pears

and

penguins

and

palm

tree.

Q

is for quack and
quail and
queue and
quill and
quaking grass

and

queen.

QUACK
QUACK

R is for rabbits, ram and Russian dancer, rose, ruin, rainbow and robin redbreast.

S

is for snowman and scarf, stork,
snowdrops, shoes
and sabots,
scorpion and

sun.

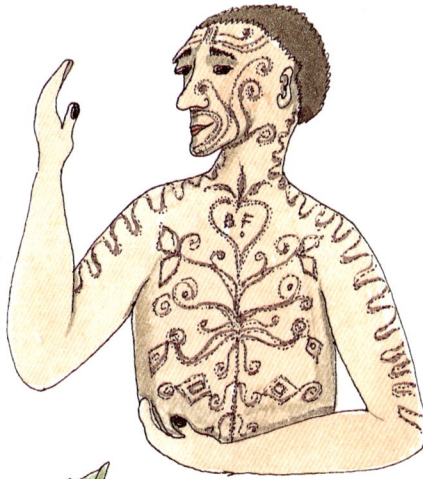

T is for travellers joy (clematis vitalba), tutu, tomahawk, tonsure, teapot, tiger, tattoo

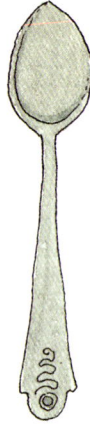

U

is for

an Ursuline nun
with an umbrella,
upside-down

urns
and
utensils.

V

is for
vehicles and viper,

viaduct, veil,
violin and

volcano.

W

is for

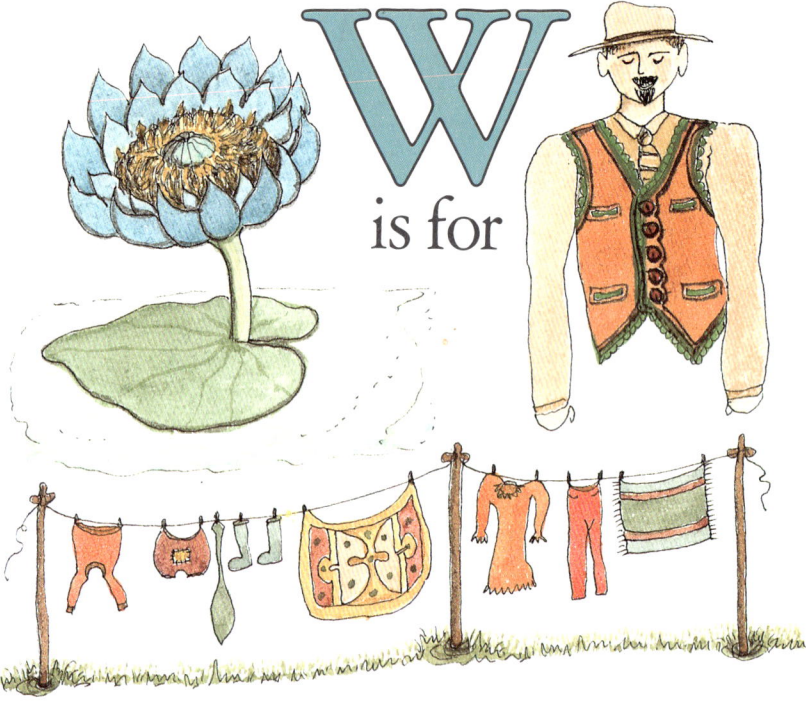

water lily, waistcoat,
watering can,
washing line,
watch and wattle.

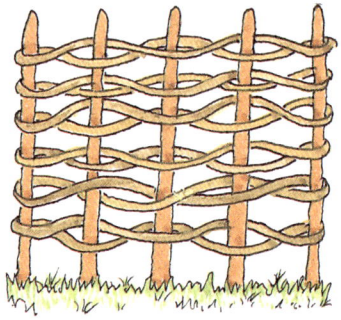

X is for   xmas tree.

XMAS LOVE

Y

is for
yacht,
yak and
yeoman, yashmaks,
yule log at yule tide.

and

Z

is for

zephyr, zebra, zorilla and zodiac.

THE ZODIAC.

The Fish — The Ram — The Bull — The Heavenly Twins — The Water Carrier — The Crab — The Goat — The Lion — The Archer — The Virgin — The Scorpion — The Scales

February — March — April — May — June — July — August — September — October — November — December — January

Taikan's favourite words

Anemone	A small wild flower found in woods
Babylonian	A person who came from the ancient civilisation of Babylon
Bust	A sculpture of the chest and head
Carp	A fresh-water fish
Dianthus	The plant family to which the pink in the picture belongs
Dromedary	A one-humped Arabian camel
Hypericum	The plant family to which the yellow flower in the picture belongs
Juno	The wife of the Roman god Jupiter
Jupiter	The chief god of the Romans; the god of gods
Kale	A cabbage with open curled leaves
Kepi	A cap worn by French soldiers
Kirk	A Scottish church

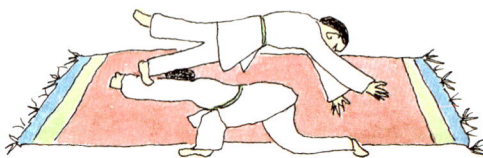

Karate	The famous art of unarmed combat from Japan
Liberty	Freedom; the statue of Liberty is in New York harbour
Llama	South American animal often used to carry things
Mangel-wurzel	A variety of beet grown for cattle
Nautilus	A shell from the Southern Seas
Neptune	Roman god of the sea

Nautch-wali	A professional dancing woman in India
Obelisk	Tall, four-sided, pointed pillar made from one stone
Orion	A constellation, or group, of seven very bright stars, three of which form Orion's belt
Quail	A type of game-bird from the partridge family
Quaking grass	A moorland grass
Sabot	A French peasant's wooden shoe
Tomahawk	A North American Indian war axe
Tonsure	The act of shaving part of the head by priests and monks
Traveller's-joy	A wild plant that grows by the roadside and is sometimes called 'old man's beard'
Tutu	A ballet dancer's short, stiff, spreading skirt
Ursuline nun	A nun who follows the teachings of Saint Ursula
Viaduct	A bridge carrying a road or railway over a valley
Viper	A type of snake
Yak	A kind of ox from Tibet
Yashmaks	A double veil worn by Muslim women, worshippers of Mohammed
Yule log	A log set alight to celebrate Christmas
Zorilla	An African skunk-like animal
Zephyr	The Greek god of the west wind

First published in 1989 by Canongate Publishing Limited,

17 Jeffrey Street, Edinburgh

© 1989 Jeanne Jeffares

British Library Cataloguing in Publication Data

Jeffares, Jeanne

Taikan's alphabet

1. English language. Readers–For children

I. Title

428.6

ISBN 0-86241-199-8

Designed by Tim Robertson

Mechanical artwork by George Studios, Edinburgh

Printed and bound in Great Britain

by MacLehose and Partners Ltd., Portsmouth